DEBITS AND CREDITS MADE EASY

A SURVIVAL GUIDE FOR YOUR FIRST WEEK IN INTRODUCTORY ACCOUNTING

D0217556

ii

DEBITS AND CREDITS MADE EASY

A SURVIVAL GUIDE FOR YOUR FIRST WEEK IN INTRODUCTORY ACCOUNTING

BY

JOHN SEBASTIAN STRANGE

www.bookstandpublishing.com

Published by
Bookstand Publishing
Morgan Hill, CA 95037
3354_3

ISBN 978-1-58909-938-8

Printed in the United States of America

iv

TABLE OF CONTENTS

LIST OF FIGURES

LIST OF FIGURES (Concluded)

INTRODUCTION

This book is designed to greatly simplify Introductory Accounting principles — debits and credits. In the typical Introductory Accounting course, you are expected to master these odd concepts by the second meeting. If you fail to understand debits and credits from the beginning, you will fall behind and struggle to catch up. Of course, failure to apply debits and credits guarantees failure on exams.

This book is not intended to be a substitute for your Introductory Accounting textbook. Rather, it is intended to be a useful supplement to guide you through the strange universe of debits and credits.

I have designed a unique system to make debits and credits understandable. With this understanding, you will have the ammunition needed when more complex topics are introduced.

Chapter 1, *Defining Terms: Debits and Credits*, defines the basic terms needed to understand the course.

Chapter 2, *Memorizing the Rules: Helpful Hints to Guide You Through the*

Maze of Debits and Credits, discusses a simplified approach to debits and credits.

Chapter 3, *Application of Terms,* illustrates the application of these principles to actual business transactions.

Remember: If you don't master debits and credits, you will find it impossible to pass your Introductory Accounting course.

CHAPTER 1

DEFINING TERMS:
DEBITS AND CREDITS

A *Debit* is the left-hand side of an account. A *Credit* is the right-hand side of an account. **DR** is the accepted abbreviation for debit; **CR** is the accepted abbreviation for credit.

Refer to **Figure 1** on page 2.

As you will note, debit (DR) does not translate as increase or decrease. Increases to assets (A), expenses (E), and drawing (D) are debited. Decreases to liabilities (L), owner's equity (OE), and revenue are also

debited (Refer to Figure 1).

FIGURE 1

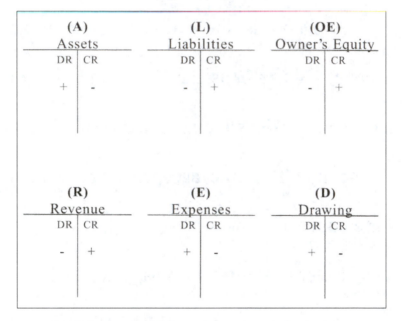

Similarly, credit (CR) does not

translate as increase or decrease. A look at

Figure 1 shows that increases to liabilities (L), owner's equity (OE), and revenue are credited; decreases to assets (A), expenses (E), and drawing (D) are also credited.

The common thread in Figure 1 is this: *Debit (DR) is always left, and Credit (CR) is always right.*

A common mistake made by Introductory Accounting students is to use the terms debit and credit in the same way they are used in the "real world." For example, if you call the customer service number for your bank, you may be told that yesterday's deposit was credited to your account — your balance has increased. You may also be told that an amount equivalent to a recent payment by check was debited from your account — your balance has decreased.

If you are to succeed in accounting, however, you must totally block these concepts from your mind. In the field of accounting, debit means left and credit means right — nothing else. Debit does not mean decrease, and credit does not mean increase. *Remember: Debit means left and credit means right.*

One final note on debits and credits before we move on to other matters: Beginning students often question why DR is the accepted abbreviation for debit, noting that there is no "r" in the word debit. The reason can be traced to the Latin origin of the word debit, which is *debere*. As you can see, there is an "r" in the word *debere*.

Assets

An asset is something you own that has value. Cash, supplies, equipment, furniture, automobiles, land, buildings, Accounts Receivable, and Prepaid Insurance are the most common assets you will use in the early stages of your Introductory Accounting course.

All but two of these terms are self-explanatory. The two terms that are probably new to you are *Accounts Receivable* and *Prepaid Insurance*.

Accounts Receivable represents amounts owed to you by customers. If a customer "charges" a product or service from you, use the Accounts Receivable account. Accounts Receivable can frequently be identified by the words "on account." If a customer buys or pays "on account," you know that you must use the Accounts Receivable account. If the customer is financing the purchase — paying in installments — the Accounts Receivable account must be used.

Prepaid Insurance should be used when you pay a premium for insurance coverage for your business. It is considered an asset because it provides a benefit — protection for your business.

Liabilities

A *liability* is a debt — an amount owed to someone else. *Accounts Payable* is the most common liability that you will encounter in the early stages of your Introductory Accounting course. Use this account when you owe money to a supplier. If you "charge" goods or services from a supplier, use Accounts Payable. This account can usually be identified by the words "on account." Thus, if you purchase or pay for goods "on account" from a supplier, be sure to use Accounts Payable. If you finance a purchase from a supplier — i.e., pay in installments — use Accounts Payable.

Many beginning students confuse Accounts Payable with Accounts Receivable. Accounts Payable is a liability — if you incur a debt to a supplier or pay off a debt to a supplier, use Accounts Payable. Accounts Receivable is an asset — if a customer owes you money or pays off an amount owed to you, use Accounts Receivable.

Owner's Equity

Owner's equity is the net worth of the business; it's what the business is worth. It is also referred to as *capital*. You can frequently spot owner's equity by the word "invest." The most common owner's equity transactions involve investment of money in the business by the owner.

Drawing

The *drawing* account is used when you take money out of the business for personal use. It is often referred to as "withdrawals."

Drawing is a temporary owner's equity account. At the end of the accounting period, all of the money in the drawing account is taken out and transferred to owner's equity. Thus, when the next accounting period starts, the balance in the drawing account will be zero.

If this procedure were not followed, you would not know how much money was taken out of the business for personal use during the current year. For example, assume that you don't close out the drawing account on December 31, 2008. When you look at the books for the year 2009, you will not know which part of the drawing represents amounts withdrawn in 2009 and which part represents amounts withdrawn in prior years. If the drawing account was not closed out on December 31, 2008, the drawing account would be overstated in the year 2009.

Revenue

Revenue is income — it is usually derived from the sale of merchandise or the providing of a service. You can usually spot revenue accounts by one of three words —

"fee," "earn," or "service." If you see any of these three words, you know that you are probably dealing with a revenue account.

Like drawing, revenue is a temporary owner's equity account. At the end of the accounting period, all of the money in the revenue account is transferred to the owner's equity account. Thus, when the next accounting period starts, the balance in the revenue accounts will be zero. If this was not done, you would not know how much revenue you earned during the current year. For example, assume that you don't close out the revenue accounts on December 31, 2008. When you look at your books for the year 2009, you will not know which part of your revenue represents income for the year 2009 and which part represents income earned in prior years. If the revenue account was not closed out on December 31, 2008, the revenue for 2009 would be overstated.

Expenses

An *expense*, like drawing and revenue, represents a temporary owner's equity account. At the end of the accounting period, all of the money in the expense account is taken out and transferred to owner's equity. If this procedure was not followed, you would not know your actual expense amounts for the current year. For example, assume that you don't close out your wage expense account on December 31, 2008. When you look at your books for the year 2009, you will not know which part of the wage expense account represents wages paid to employees in 2009 and which part represents amounts paid in prior years.

The most common expenses that you will encounter in the early stages of your

Introductory Accounting course are *wage expense*, *rent expense*, and *utilities expense* (e.g., telephone and electricity).

Be careful not to confuse expenses with liabilities. As I mentioned earlier, expenses are temporary owner's equity accounts — they are closed out (zeroed out) at the end of the accounting period. Therefore, the balance in each expense account will be zero at the start of the next accounting period.

Liabilities, on the other hand, do not get closed out at the end of the accounting period. Remember that liabilities are debts. If you owe someone money at the close of business on December 31, 2008, you still owe that same person money on January 1, 2009 — the start of the next accounting period. Be sure to memorize the most common expenses that you will see in the early stages of your Introductory Accounting course — *wage expense, rent expense,* and *utilities expense.*

CHAPTER 2

MEMORIZING THE RULES: HELPFUL HINTS TO GUIDE YOU THROUGH THE MAZE OF DEBITS AND CREDITS

In any Introductory Accounting course, you will encounter an illustration showing the rules for debits and credits. Refer to **Figure 2** on page 20.

It is absolutely essential to memorize the rules in Figure 2 immediately. *Remember: DR is the commonly abbreviated form for debit; CR is the commonly abbreviated form for credit.*

FIGURE 2

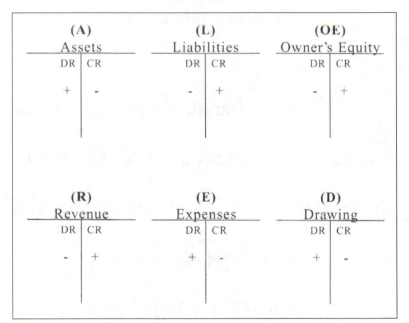

To simplify memorization, use "A" for assets, "L" for liabilities, "OE" for owner's equity (also known as *capital*), "R" for revenue, "E" for expenses, and "D" for drawing.

This will bring us to **Rule #1**: *Each of the "ADE" accounts — "A" for assets, "D" for drawing, "E" for expenses — will show the following:*

Refer to **Figure 3** on page 22.

Figure 3 shows the rules for the ADE accounts — assets, drawing, expenses — which first appeared in Figure 1.

FIGURE 3

(A) Assets		(D) Drawing		(E) Expenses	
DR	CR	DR	CR	DR	CR
+	-	+	-	+	-

To put it simply, remember that increases to assets, drawing, and expenses — the "ADE" accounts — are always debited. Decreases to assets, drawing, and expenses — the "ADE" accounts — are always credited.

This brings us to **Rule #2**: *If you are not dealing with an "ADE" account (assets,* *drawing, expenses) — in other words, if you are dealing with a liability, owner's equity, or revenue account — you must do the following:*

Refer to **Figure 4** on page 24.

The rules shown in Figure 4 relate to liabilities, owner's equity, and revenue; these first appeared in Figure 1.

To put it simply, remember that increases to liabilities, owner's equity, and revenue are always credited; decreases to liabilities, owner's equity, and revenue are always debited.

FIGURE 4

(L) Liabilities		(OE) Owner's Equity		(R) Revenue	
DR	CR	DR	CR	DR	CR
-	+	-	+	-	+

To sum up Rules 1 and 2: *When you are dealing with an "ADE" account (asset, drawing, expense), increases are always debited and decreases are always credited. If you are not dealing with an "ADE"* account *(liability, owner's equity, revenue),* *do the opposite — increases are always credited and decreases are always debited.*

This brings us to **Rule #3**: *It is very unusual to decrease a "RED" account — R for revenue, E for expense, and D for drawing.*

To illustrate, let's refer to **Figure 5** on page 26.

The rules in Figure 5 involve revenue, expense, and drawing accounts; these first appeared in Figure 1.

FIGURE 5

(R) Revenue		(E) Expenses		(D) Drawing	
DR	CR	DR	CR	DR	CR
-	+	+	-	+	-

To simplify Rule #3, remember that a debit (minus) to a revenue account is very unusual — and that it is very unusual to credit (minus) an expense or drawing account. With this in mind, remember that revenue accounts are almost always credited, and that expense and drawing accounts are almost always debited.

Unless you are making a correcting entry or a period-ending closing entry, Rule #3 will always hold true: Revenue accounts will always be credited — they are never debited. Expenses and drawing accounts will always be debited — they are never credited. (Correcting entries and period-ending closing entries are topics that are covered in detail in the later phases of a traditional Introductory Accounting course).

CHAPTER 3

APPLICATION OF TERMS

In this chapter, we will apply the rules for debits and credits to the types of business transactions that are commonly encountered in the first week of an Introductory Accounting course.

First, let's look at the illustration that first appeared in Chapter 1, repeated here as **Figure 6** on page 30. These are the rules for debits and credits, which were discussed earlier.

FIGURE 6

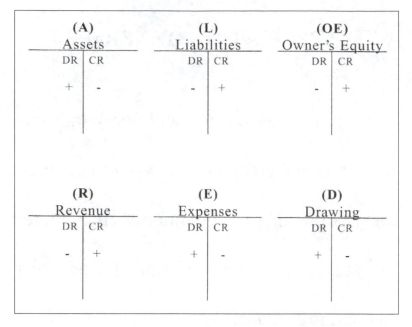

Now, let's apply these rules to our first transaction.

Transaction #1: Jane Doe, owner, invests $50,000 in business

Refer to **Figure 7** on page 32 to see how this transaction was recorded. In this transaction, you will note that cash is debited.

Now, refer to the rule for assets in **Figure 8** on page 32.

Because cash is an asset, and because investing cash in the business increases cash, we debit the account. Many beginning students mistakenly credit cash, perhaps in the belief that Jane Doe personally has less

cash.

FIGURE 7

(ASSETS)		(OWNER'S EQUITY)	
Cash		Jane Doe, Capital	
DR	CR	DR	CR
50,000			50,000

FIGURE 8

(A)		(OE)	
Assets		Owner's Equity	
DR	CR	DR	CR
+	-	-	+

However, in the field of accounting, we use the *Business Entity* concept: We are concerned with effects on the business — not the individual owner. If Jane Doe invests cash in the business, the business has more cash. Remembering that cash is an asset, the rule is: *Increase an asset, debit the account.*

As I mentioned in Chapter 1, you can usually spot owner's equity (or capital) by the word "invest." Remembering that owner's equity represents what the business is worth, Jane Doe's business is worth more due to the fact that she invested money in the business.

Now, refer to the rule for owner's equity in Figure 8.

Because the business is worth more, owner's equity increases. The rule is this: *Increase owner's equity (or capital), credit the account.*

Before we move on to the next transaction, note that the debit of $50,000.00 equals the credit of $50,000.00.

For every business transaction, debits must always equal credits.

Transaction #2: Jane Doe, owner,

withdraws $1,000.00 from business for

personal use

Refer to **Figure 9** below to see how this transaction is recorded.

FIGURE 9

Jane Doe, Drawing		(ASSETS) Cash	
DR	CR	DR	CR
1000			1000

Whenever you withdraw money from the business for personal use, automatically debit the drawing account.

Drawing is one of the "RED" accounts discussed earlier; it is very unusual to have a "minus" to a "RED" account.

Now, refer to **Figure 10** below to review the rule for drawing.

FIGURE 10

(D) Drawing		(A) Assets	
DR	CR	DR	CR
+	-	+	-

Because it is very unusual to have a "minus" to a "RED" account, it is very unusual to credit the drawing account.

36

Unless you are making a period-ending closing entry or a correcting entry, don't credit drawing.

If cash is withdrawn from the business, the business has less cash. Remember that in accounting we are concerned with the books of the business — not the individual owner.

Because cash is an asset, refer to the rule for assets in Figure 10.

Notice that decreases to assets are credited. We credit cash because we are taking cash out of the business — decrease an asset, credit the account.

Transaction #3: Purchased supplies on account, $500.00

We record this transaction in **Figure 11** below.

If you purchase supplies, you have more supplies. Remember that supplies are an asset.

FIGURE 11

(ASSETS) Supplies		(LIABILITIES) Accounts Payable	
DR	CR	DR	CR
500			500

The rule for assets can be found in **Figure 12** below.

FIGURE 12

(A) Assets		(L) Liabilities	
DR	CR	DR	CR
+	-	-	+

Referring to Figure 12, you can see that an increase in an asset is debited. Thus, we debit supplies for $500.00.

If you see the words "on account," this means that either Accounts Receivable or

Accounts Payable is affected. A purchase of supplies on account indicates that you have "charged" the supplies on your charge account — no cash has been given. As you know, when you "charge" a product or service, your debts go up. In accounting, debts are referred to as liabilities.

Now, let's refer to the rule for liabilities in Figure 12.

If you owe money to a supplier, you should use Accounts Payable. Remember that when you charge a produce or service, your debts — liabilities — increase.

Because the Liability Accounts Payable has increased, we credit the account.

Transaction #4: Refer to Transaction #3 —

Assume that thirty days later you pay on

account the amount owed

We record this transaction in **Figure 13** below.

FIGURE 13

(LIABILITIES) Accounts Payable		(ASSETS) Cash	
DR	CR	DR	CR
500			500

Remember: "On account" means that either Accounts Receivable or Accounts Payable is affected. Notice that you are paying money to another person. Because you are the one who is paying out cash, it logically follows that you must owe money to that person.

If someone else owed you money, he or she would be paying you. Because you owe the money, the Liability Accounts Payable is affected. You are paying off an Accounts Payable. You are paying off a debt — a liability.

Because Accounts Payable is a liability, let's review the rule for liabilities in **Figure 14** below.

FIGURE 14

Liabilities		Assets	
DR	CR	DR	CR
-	+	+	-

Paying off the Accounts Payable reduces this liability account. Referring to Figure 14, we can see that a reduction in a liability requires a debit; therefore, we debit Accounts Payable.

You are paying cash to a supplier. Whenever you see the words "pay," "pays," or "paid," cash is definitely affected. Because cash is an asset, let's review the rules for assets in Figure 14.

The payment of cash to a supplier reduces your cash. As Figure 14 shows, a reduction in an asset is credited. To sum it up, if you pay cash, you have less cash — decrease the asset cash, credit the account.

Transaction #5: Earned fees on account,

$1,000.00

Refer to **Figure 15** below to see how this transaction is recorded.

FIGURE 15

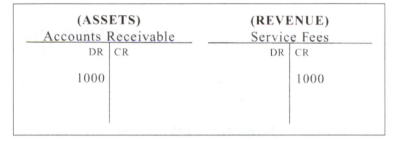

Once again, you will notice the words "on account" have appeared. Remember that these words indicate that either Accounts

Receivable or Accounts Payable is affected. Earning fees on account can be interpreted as follows: You have performed $1,000.00 worth of services for a customer (or client). The customer charged the services — you have not been paid. Therefore, the customer owes you $1,000.00. When a customer owes you money, the Asset Accounts Receivable is affected. The amount owed to you by customers — Accounts Receivable — has been increased.

Let's refer to the rule for assets in **Figure 16** on page 47.

FIGURE 16

(A) Assets		(R) Revenue	
DR	CR	DR	CR
+	-	-	+

As you can see in the above illustration, an increase in an asset is debited. Therefore, the increase in the Asset Accounts Receivable is debited to reflect the increase in the account.

As mentioned earlier, the words "fee," "earn," and "service" normally indicate that a revenue account is affected.

Be sure to use an appropriate title —
"Service Fees," "Client Fees," "Professional
Fees," etc. — for the account. The title on
the account will depend upon the type of
business and its services. For example, a law
firm would most likely use "Professional
Fees" or "Client Fees," while a lawn service
would most likely use "Service Fees." Let's
assume that we are dealing with a lawn
service — we will use "Service Fees."
Earning fees indicates that revenue has
increased.

Let's review the rules for revenue accounts in Figure 16.

As you can see, the rule is: *Increase Revenue, credit the account.* Because we have an increase in the revenue account service fees, we record a credit.

Also, it is worth remembering that revenue accounts are "RED" accounts. As previously stated, it is very unusual to debit a revenue account. (It is very unusual to have a "minus" to a "RED" account — in this case, the "minus" would be a debit.) Unless you are dealing with a period-ending closing entry or correcting an error, revenue accounts should always be credited.

Transaction #6: Refer to Transaction #5 — One month later customer pays on account the amount owed

Refer to **Figure 17** on Page 51 to see how this transaction is recorded.

Anytime you see the word "pays," cash is involved.

Refer to **Figure 18** on Page 51.

As you can see, an increase to an asset is debited. Because the customer is paying you cash, you have more cash; and because cash is an asset, you debit cash to reflect the

increase in cash.

FIGURE 17

(ASSETS) Cash		(ASSETS) Accounts Receivable	
DR	CR	DR	CR
1000			1000

FIGURE 18

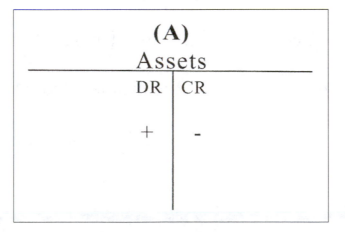

(A) Assets	
DR	CR
+	-

Notice the words "on account." As mentioned earlier, these words indicate that either Accounts Receivable or Accounts Payable is affected. If a customer pays on account, it indicates that he or she owes you money. When a customer owes you money, Accounts Receivable is affected. Remembering that Accounts Receivable is an asset, refer to Figure 18.

Because the customer has paid off his or her Accounts Receivable, the Asset Accounts Receivable has been reduced. As

Figure 18 shows, a decrease in an asset must be credited.

Because the payment by the customer reduces the Accounts Receivable, we credit the account.

Transaction #7: Paid a $1,000.00 premium on a business insurance policy

Refer to **Figure 19** below.

FIGURE 19

(ASSETS) Pre-Paid Insurance		(ASSETS) Cash	
DR	CR	DR	CR
1000			1000

The premiums paid on a business-related insurance policy represent an asset — prepaid insurance. These premiums provide a benefit for your business — insurance coverage. In this situation, you have more insurance coverage — more prepaid insurance. If you don't pay your premiums, you have less insurance coverage; you actually lose your insurance.

Refer to **Figure 20** on page 55.

Remember that payment of an insurance premium gives you more insurance coverage — not less. Therefore, there has been an increase in the asset prepaid insurance. Because increases in assets are debited, we debit the prepaid insurance account.

FIGURE 20

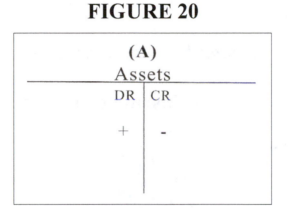

The word "paid" indicates that cash is involved. Remember that cash is an asset. Refer to Figure 20.

As you can see, a decrease in an asset is credited. Because you have paid cash to the insurance company, you have less cash. Therefore, we must credit the cash account to reflect the decrease in cash.

Transaction #8: Paid rent, $1,000.00

We record this transaction in **Figure 21** below.

FIGURE 21

(E)		(ASSETS)	
Rent Expense		Cash	
DR	CR	DR	CR
1000			1000

Rent paid to a landlord represents an expense.

Refer to **Figure 22** below.

FIGURE 22

(E) Expenses		(A) Assets	
DR	CR	DR	CR
+	-	+	-

As mentioned earlier, expenses are one of the "RED" accounts. Remember that it is very unusual to have a "minus" to a "RED" account. It is very unusual to credit an expense account; this type of account should only be credited when you make a correcting entry or an end-of-period closing entry.

When you pay an expense, you automatically debit the account. Therefore, rent expense must be debited.

Remember that the word "paid" indicates that cash is involved. Because cash is an asset, refer to Figure 22.

A payment of rent to your landlord reduces the asset cash. The rule is: *Decrease an asset, credit the account.* Therefore, cash must be credited.

Transaction #9: Sold equipment for cash, $5,000.00

We record this transaction in **Figure 23** below.

FIGURE 23

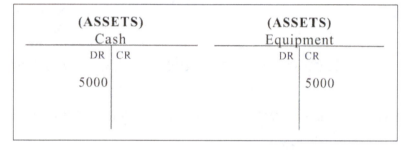

If you sell equipment for cash, you have received cash. Cash is an asset. Refer to **Figure 24** on Page 60.

FIGURE 24

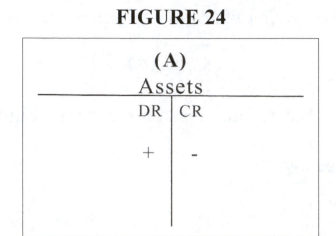

Remember, the rule is: *Increase an asset, debit the account.* If you received cash, you have more cash. Because cash is an asset, we debit the account.

If you sell equipment, you have less equipment. Equipment is an asset. Refer to Figure 24.

If you sell equipment, the asset equipment is decreased. The rule is: *Decrease an asset, credit the account.* Therefore, we credit the equipment account.

Transaction #10: Purchased furniture for cash, $1,000.00

We record this transaction in **Figure 25** on page 62. Furniture is an asset. If you purchase furniture, you have more furniture. Refer to **Figure 26** on page 62.

FIGURE 25

(ASSETS) Furniture				(ASSETS) Cash	
DR	CR			DR	CR
1000					1000

FIGURE 26

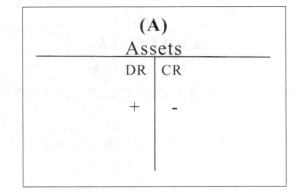

(A) Assets	
DR	CR
+	-

The rule is: *Increase an asset, debit the account.* Because we have purchased furniture, the increase in this asset must be recorded as a debit.

If you purchase furniture for cash, you have spent cash. If you spend cash, you have less cash. Remember that cash is an asset.

Refer to the rule for assets in Figure 26.

Spending cash for the furniture results in a decrease in the asset cash. The rule is: *Decrease an asset, credit the account.* Therefore, we credit the cash account.

CONCLUSION

You have just read a simplified guide to the world of debits and credits. Debits and credits are an integral part of any Introductory Accounting course. With an understanding of the basic concepts discussed in this book, you can tackle the more complex transactions that you will later encounter.

Good Luck!

ABOUT THE AUTHOR

John Sebastian Strange has been the Accounting Chairperson for the Evening/ Saturday Division of the College of Westchester, White Plains, New York, since 1992. He has 25 years of teaching experience, and is listed in *Who's Who Among America's Teachers*. He is a member of the National Society of Accountants and the American Accounting Association.

NOTES

CPSIA information can be obtained
at www.ICGtesting.com
Printed in the USA
BVHW040348260719
554320BV00004B/380/P